Welcome to Poland

By Patrick Ryan

The Child's World®

Published by The Child's World®
1980 Lookout Drive
Mankato, MN 56003-1705
800-599-READ
www.childsworld.com

Content Adviser: M. B. B. Biskupski, Blejwas Endowed Chair in Polish History,
Department of History, Central Connecticut State University, New Britain, CT
Design and Production: The Creative Spark, San Juan Capistrano, CA
Editorial: Publisher's Diner, Wendy Mead, Greenwich, CT
Photo Research: Deborah Goodsite, Califon, NJ

Cover and title page photo: Mirek Weichsel/First Light/Jupiterimages
Interior photos: Alamy: 7 bottom (lookGaleria), 10 (Arco Images), 24 (Caro), 27 (les polders);
Animals Animals/Earth Scenes: 3 middle, 8 (Gerard Lacz), 3 bottom, 16 (Manfred Gottschalk); AP
Photo: 25 (Czarek Sokolowski); Art Resource: 12 (Erich Lessing); The Bridgeman Art Library: 11
(Wladislaw II Jageillon (1351-1434) Grand Duke of Lithuania (engraving), Lesser, Aleksander
(1814–84)/Bibliotheque Polonaise, Paris, France, Bonora); Corbis: 9 (Adrian Arbib); Getty Images:
6 (De Agostini), 7 top (Piotr Jamski), 13 (AFP), 18, 23 (Piotr Malecki/Liaison); iStockphoto.com:
22 (ShyMan), 26 (fotohmmm), 28 (Ufuk Zivana), 29 (Adam Korzekwa); Lonely Planet Images: 31
(Krzysztof Dydynski); NASA Earth Observatory: 4 (Reto Stockli); Panos Pictures: 17 (Mikkel
Ostergaard), 19 (Piotr Malecki); Peter Arnold, Inc.: 20 (Peter Hirth), 21, 30 (Ullstein-CARO/Bastian);
Photolibrary Group: 3 top, 14.
Map: XNR Productions: 5

Library of Congress Cataloging-in-Publication Data
Ryan, Patrick, 1948–
   Welcome to Poland / by Patrick Ryan.
      p. cm. — (Welcome to the world)
   Includes bibliographical references and index.
   ISBN 978-1-59296-974-6 (alk. paper)
   1. Poland—Juvenile literature.   I. Title. II. Series.

DK4147.R973 2008
943.8—dc22

2007034775

Contents

Where Is Poland?

Imagine flying high above Earth in a hot air balloon. You could look down and see lots of things that you do not see every day. As you passed over the Atlantic Ocean, you could look down on the **continent** of Europe. A continent is a large body of land. Europe is speckled with many countries. One of these countries is Poland.

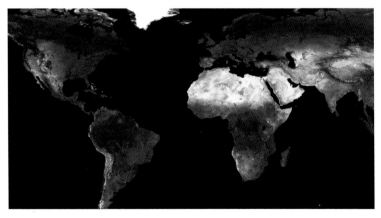

This picture gives us a flat look at Earth. Poland is inside the red circle.

Did you **know?**

Poland is really called "The Republic of Poland." People just say "Poland" for short.

LITHUANIA

Baltic Sea

Gulf of Gdansk

RUSSIA

Gdansk

Szczecin

BELARUS

Lake Beldany

Masurian Lakes

POLAND

⊛ National capital

● Other city

▲ Mountain peak

⊛ Warsaw

Łodz

Polkowice

ERMANY

Wrocław

Sudeten Mountains

Bledowska Desert

Katowice

Krakow

UKRAINE

N

W E

S

CZECH
REPUBLIC

Carpathian Mountains

▲ *Rysy Peak*

0   30   60 miles

0   30   60 kilometers

AUSTRIA

SLOVAKIA

The Land

The name *Poland* means "land of fields." That is because most of the country is low and flat. But in the south, tall mountains can be found. These are the Sudeten and Carpathian Mountains. Some of these mountains are so tall that snow covers their tops all of the time. Poland's highest mountain is Rysy Peak. It is more than 8,000 feet (2,438 meters) high.

Poland's flatlands are great for farming such crops as wheat, potatoes, and other vegetables.

Poland has many neighbors. To the north lie Russia, Lithuania, and the beautiful Baltic Sea. Slovakia and the Czech Republic border Poland to the south. Belarus and the Ukraine touch Poland on the east, and Germany lies to the west.

Part of the Carpathian Mountains are called the Tatra Mountains.

Did you know?

The Bledowska Desert is located in the center of Poland. It is home to the only sand dunes in all of Europe.

7

Plants and Animals

Many types of animals live in Poland. Such creatures as marmots and chamois (SHAM-ee) make their homes in the high Carpathian Mountains. Marmots look a lot like the woodchucks that live in many American forests. Chamois are small antelope that are only about as big as a goat.

A marmot snacks on a flower.

The forests of Poland are home to wolves, bears, wild pigs, and the last European bison. During World War II, all of the bison in Poland were killed. Later, the government brought them back by releasing some bison raised in zoos into the wild.

This Polish forest is filled with wild garlic.

Birch, spruce, maple, beech, and oak trees all grow well in Poland. Many kinds of flowers, short grasses, and other plants can be found there, too. Edelweiss (AY-dull-vys) is a pretty flower that grows in Poland's high mountain areas. It is star-shaped with fuzzy white petals.

Long Ago

The land that is now Poland has been home to people for thousands of years. The early people we know the most about are the **Slavs.** For many years, these early settlers

Sculptures of the Slavs stand by the shore of Lake Beldany.

formed groups and fought against each other for control of different areas. Then one family, the Piast family, united the groups together as one country.

Years later, the country of Lithuania joined with Poland to create a huge state. In fact, during the 1400s, Poland was the largest country in Europe.

Wladyslaw II served as king of Poland from 1386 to 1434 and helped unite Poland and Lithuania.

Over time, Poland became involved in wars with other countries. About 200 years ago, all of Poland was taken over by other countries. Poland was no longer its own country! This angered many Poles, who wanted their own leaders. Finally, after years of fighting and talking, Poland became a country again in 1918.

Poland Today

Of all of the groups that attacked Poland, the most feared were the **Nazis** from Germany. The Nazis believed that

The city of Gdansk was badly damaged during World War II.

certain people, races, and religions were better than others. They also believed the government of a country should have complete control over people's lives. Many countries were afraid the Nazis would cause trouble. Nazi troops invaded Poland in September 1939. This led to the start of World War II. Soon after the war began, Russian troops also entered Poland.

After years of fighting, World War II finally ended in 1945. Many of Poland's beautiful buildings had been destroyed, and over 6 million Poles were dead.

Part of Poland was given to Russia after the war. The Poles weren't happy with this. They wanted freedom and their own government. In 1980, a man named Lech Walesa formed a political party to help form a new Poland. When **communism** fell in 1989, Poland was finally free!

Lech Walesa (center) gives a speech to a crowd of supporters.

Girls posing in traditional Polish outfits

The People

Poles are a proud people. Even after years of fighting and suffering, they have kept the **traditions,** or ways of life, that are special to them. Poles also have kept their language, even though other countries once ruled their land. The country experienced terrible losses in World War II. More than 6 million Poles died during the war.

Family, friends, and education are very important to the Polish people, too. They love to spend time with their loved ones and share a laugh or two.

Did you know?

One Polish tradition is called the "Drowning of Marzanna." Every spring, Poles make a dummy out of straw. The dummy represents Marzanna, the symbol of winter. They dress it up and drop it into the nearest river or lake. This is a fun way for Poles to mark the end of winter and the coming of spring.

Polish cities, such as Gdansk, are busy places.

City Life and Country Life

Most of Poland's people live in small cities or towns. Many live in simple apartments with two or three bedrooms. Poland's cities are much like those in the United States, with buildings, shops, and restaurants.

A son rides home with his father after working in the fields.

In the countryside, people live a simple life. They live in cottages made out of brick or wood. Most country people are farmers who work on the flat plains. They grow such crops as potatoes, fruits, vegetables, and wheat.

Schools and Language

Children in Poland must go to school between the ages of 7 and 15. Just like American children, they learn reading, math, and science. When Poland gained its freedom in 1989, the people worked hard to make sure children could get a good education. Books were updated and more teachers were hired. Education is very important to the Polish people.

A student gets help from the teacher during math class.

A young boy reads a Polish newspaper.

Polish is the official language of Poland. There are also different **dialects** of Polish in certain areas of the country. That means a person speaking Polish in the northern part of the country may sound different from someone in the south.

A car factory in Polkowice

Work

Less than 100 years ago, most of the people in Poland worked on farms. Today, many people work in factories that produce things to sell. Cars and big machines are just two of the products made in Poland's huge factories.

These workers help take care of a company's computer system.

Other people work on farms or in the country's coal mines. Many Poles have jobs just like those in the United States. Restaurants, banks, shops, and offices are all places where Polish people work hard.

Food

Pierogies stuffed with meat

"Would you like some zupa?" *Zupa* is soup and the Polish people love it. They also enjoy dishes with lots of meats and vegetables. *Pierogies* (peh-ROH-geez) are another favorite food. They are dumplings filled with different meats, cheeses, and vegetables such as cabbage or potatoes.

Since Poland is in the middle of Europe, dishes from other European countries are popular, too. German, French, and Italian foods can all be found on Polish tables.

A family enjoys a meal of *zupa,* or soup, together.

You can find children playing soccer all over Poland, from the cities to small towns.

Pastimes

Soccer! Soccer! Soccer! Each year thousands of young people in Poland play soccer. Their goal is to someday make the national team and play in the World Cup. Poland's team has made it to the World Cup many times, and finished third in 1982 and in 1974.

The Polish people love to be outside. Besides soccer, other popular pastimes include skiing and fishing. They love nearly anything else that takes them outdoors!

Some children take a break from their skiing lesson.

Holidays

Polish Easter eggs

Religious holidays are very important in Poland. Most Polish people belong to the Roman Catholic faith, and the most important holidays are Christmas and Easter. Christmas is celebrated from December 6 all the way through December 26. It is a happy time when Polish families celebrate and spend time with each other. Easter is a favorite holiday for the children. Much like Easter in the United States, children paint Easter eggs with beautiful designs.

Would you like to visit Poland someday? Perhaps you might see a chamois or watch a soccer game. You might sample some Polish soup or even climb the Carpathian Mountains. You'll find plenty of interesting things to see and do in Poland!

Children show buildings they made for a Christmas contest.

Fast Facts About Poland

Area: Almost 121,000 square miles (313,000 square kilometers)—a little smaller than New Mexico.

Population: About 39 million people

Capital City: Warsaw

Other Important Cities: Gdansk and Krakow

Money: The zloty

National Language: Polish

National Holidays: Constitution Day on May 3 and Independence Day on November 11

National Flag: Two stripes of white and red

Head of Government: The prime minister

Head of State: The president

Famous People:

Frédéric Chopin: composer of classical music

Ignacy Paderewski: composer and former prime minister of Poland

John Paul II: former pope, or leader, of the Roman Catholic Church

Lech Walesa: labor activist and former president of Poland

Marie Curie: Nobel Prize-winning scientist

Nicholaus Copernicus: astronomer, scientist who studies the skies

Queen Jadwiga: Queen of Poland in the 1300s and later became a saint

National Song: *"Mazurek Dabrowskiego"* (Dabrowski's Mazurka)

Poland has not yet succumbed.
As long as we remain,
What the foe by force has seized,
Sword in hand we'll gain.

March! March, Dabrowski!
March from Italy to Poland!
Under your command
We shall reach our land.

Cross the Vistula and Warta
And the Poles we shall be;
We've been shown by Bonaparte
Ways to victory.

March! March, Dabrowski!
March from Italy to Poland!

Under your command
We shall reach our land.

As Czarniecki Poznan town
    regains.
Fighting with the Swede,
To free our fatherland from
    chains.
We shall return by sea.

March! March, Dabrowski!
March from Italy to Poland!
Under your command
We shall reach our land.

Father, in tears, says to his
    Basia:

"Just listen,
It seems that our people
Are beating the drums."

March! March, Dabrowski!
March from Italy to Poland!
Under your command
We shall reach our land.

Warsaw is the capital of Poland.

Polish Folktale: The Legend of the White Eagle

Many years ago, three brothers, Lech, Czech, and Rus, set out with their troops to find new lands.
After traveling together for some time, they decided to split up and go in three different directions.
Czech went to the left. Rus went to the right. Lech went straight ahead. He traveled down a mountain
and across the plains. One day while in a meadow, Lech spotted a beautiful white eagle overhead.
He watched as the bird settled in its nest high atop a rock. Soon Lech decided that this area would
be the new home for his people and called it *Gniezno*—eagle's nest. For a long time, the white
eagle has been a symbol of Poland.

29

How Do You Say...

ENGLISH	POLISH	HOW TO SAY IT
hello	dzien dobry	JEN DOH-brey
good-bye	do widzenia	DOH veed-ZEN-yuh
please	proze	PRROH-sheh
thank you	dziekuje	JEN-KOO-yah
one	jeden	YEH-den
two	dwa	DVAH
three	trzy	CHY
Poland	Polska	PULL-ska

Glossary

communism (KAHM-yoo-nih-zem)
Communism is an idea that some
governments use to rule their countries.
Governments that practice communism
believe that property should belong to the
whole country instead of individual people.

continent (KON-tih-nent) Most of the
land areas on Earth are divided up into
huge sections called continents. Some
continents contain many countries. Poland
is located on the continent of Europe.

dialects (DYE-uh-lekts) A dialect is
a different form of a language. There are
different dialects of Polish in certain areas
of the country.

Nazis (NAHT-zeez) The Nazis were a
political group that believed certain people,
races, and religions were better than others.
When the Nazis invaded Poland in 1939,
World War II began.

religious (ree-LIH-juss) When
something is religious, it deals with
thoughts and beliefs about God. Religious
holidays are very important in Poland.

Slavs (SLAHVZ) The Slavs were a group
of people who lived in Poland long ago.
They are the ancestors of today's Poles.

traditions (truh-DIH-shunz) Traditions
are ways of doing things. The Polish people
have kept many of their traditions from
long ago.

Further Information

Read It

Everett, Charles and Barbara Everett. *The Changing Face of Poland.* London: Hodder Wayland, 2005.

Mulla-Feroze, Umaima and Paul Grajnert. *Welcome to Poland.* Milwaukee, WI: Gareth Stevens, 2003.

Nichols, Jeremy and Emilia Trembicka-Nichols. *Poland.* London: Evans, 2005.

Look It Up

Visit our Web page for lots of links about Poland:
http://www.childsworld.com/links

Note to Parents, Teachers, and Librarians: We routinely verify our Web links to make sure they are safe, active sites—so encourage your readers to check them out!

Index